From Mourning to Morning

Putting on the Garment of Praise

Angela R. Curtis

Copyright © 2006 by Angela R. Curtis

From Mourning to Morning
Putting on the Garment of Praise
by Angela R. Curtis

Printed in the United States of America

ISBN 1-60034-683-9

All rights reserved solely by the author. The author guarantees all contents are original and do not infringe upon the legal rights of any other person or work. No part of this book may be reproduced in any form without the permission of the author. The views expressed in this book are not necessarily those of the publisher.

Unless otherwise indicated, Bible quotations are taken from New Century Version of the Bible. Copyright © 1987, 1988, 1991 by Word Publishing, a division of Thomas Nelson, Inc.

Illustrations by Golden D. Shelton.

www.xulonpress.com

Dedication

I dedicate this book to the memory of our son, Brian Edwin Curtis II. You were mommy's and daddy's little blessing for such a time as this. Your presence brought us unspeakable joy. You lived up to your name, for you were a *strong man*. Tell Great Grandma Hill, Great Grandma Jackson, and Grandpa Fields we say hello. We will see you again.

Foreword

Angie,

    With much joy in my heart, I tell you that I am honored that you asked me to read this God-inspired work. Truly, the Lord cares for His people—this truth is evident by the lives you and Brian live!

    Up to now, I knew of only one teacher who God anointed to teach through personal pain and tears; but now (Lord, be magnified), I know two more—you and Brian.

    God uniquely certified, qualified, and sanctified this timely work. Being the good stewards that you are, you've placed God's treasure in this earthen vessel—*From Mourning to Morning*, helping others to:

- Expose hurts and pains that many people experience, yet fail to reveal; it is regrettable that some think God stopped caring for them—but "M2M" is their balm;
- Confront the enemy with a ROD (Revelation of Deliverance);
- Allow tears that flow now to water and grow their ministry and service to God;
- Comfort the brokenhearted;
- Revive the joy of Jesus in their lives; and
- Declare that it's Morning Time, again!

Father,

    We honor You and we adore Your Son, our Savior Jesus Christ! Thank you for the peace that surpasses all understanding—time and time again! You're worthy—only You!
    Oh Lord, our Lord, How Excellent is Your Name in all the earth!
    Glory to Your matchless name!

Your Elder Brother,

RD

Endorsement

Dear Angela,

    I praise God for you and your family. I have been blessed to witness the presence of God in your life through very challenging seasons. I am personally proud of your faith in these challenging seasons. When you told me you were writing a book, I knew deep in my spirit the book would be a part of your transition and transformation. I have seen major transitions in your life and ministry. Transitions involve three phases. These phases are closure, change, and new beginnings. Your book *From Mourning to Morning* addresses the pain of transition. Psalm 30:5 states, "Weeping may endure for the night but joy cometh in the morning." God has taken your pain and carved out a precious stone. This book is one of those precious stones from the heart. This book will bless multitudes. *From Mourning to Morning* will bring closure to open wounds—wounds of hurt, failure, disappointment, and heartbreak. *From Mourning to Morning* will push many people into their new beginning. You have demonstrated that "joy does come in the morning."

K.A. Williams
Kingdom Harvest International Church
Richmond, Virginia

Acknowledgements

I would like to thank my Abba Father, my Lord and Savior Jesus Christ, and the Holy Spirit for birthing this work in me. It is with their guidance from above that I am here today to share my heart with you. I would like to thank the priest of my house, the love of my life, my husband, Brian Curtis. Brian, you know the story well, but because He lives we can face tomorrow. Thank you is not enough to say. I thank God for your covering, prayers, and unconditional love. Love ya "B." I would like to thank my family, in particular, my niece Niya Proctor. Niya, not only do you make auntie laugh, but a little child shall lead them. I truly thank God for my spiritual family, the saints of the most high at Kingdom Harvest International Church (KHIC). Bishop Kevin A. Williams, Sr., and Pastor Michele Williams, words cannot express the heartfelt love I have for you and our ministry. Eyes truly have not seen nor have ears heard what God is doing, has done, and continues to do in our ministry and in your personal lives. To Elder Harrison and Cheryl, my brotha and sistah, thanks for caring and being there when I need you the most. I know you got my back. To Golden Shelton, Master Stylist and illustrator extraordinaire, I could not have done this without you. May the Lord continue to bless and keep you. To brother Rick Williams, I thank God for using you to put the rhythm to the rhyme—an anointed minstrel you are. To the Nabrits, your family is such an inspiration to Brian and me. Paula, only God knows how much your encouragement and mentoring mean. Thanks for all you do. To Gail M. Oliver, we started out as co-workers and ended as friends. To the Beltway Bandits, you know who you are—I thank God for each and every one of you. To Elder Randy "RD" and Sister Gwen Davis, you are such a godly example. Continue to do what you do. Sister Glenice "G," you know God sent you on a mission; I just did not know that I was a part of it. Deacon Niketa, thanks for your timely advice. To Xulon Press, I thank God for the vision the Lord has given to you. Thank you for allowing Christian authors to have a place to express what God has placed on their hearts. To every prayer warrior, interceder, encourager, and friend of God, thank you. You are too numerous to name, but please know that I appreciate you and all that you do.

To all that will read these words, thank you for moving from mourning to praise. Remember, no matter where you find yourselves, God is the lifter of your head, and He is more than able to perform just what He said!

Prologue

From Joy to Pain—Pain to Praise

The joy began when we found out that we were pregnant. It was February 2000. The previous years had been filled with the sickness and death of my father, grandmother, aunt, and uncle. A new millennium, a new blessing, a new thing. Who could ask for more than that! All of the speaking those things that be not, as though they were, had finally manifested. I was only a month pregnant, but when the confirmation was given that we were going to be parents, a new type of joy filled my soul. What I had been praying about, fasting about, had finally come true. Wow, it was truly exhilarating. Brian, my husband, went directly into protection mode. It was so sweet. No one on earth knew that this wonderful journey would turn onto a street called tears. The pregnancy was uneventful until about the second trimester. I was sent to more tests than I knew existed. For this first-time mother, it was a walk of faith. Faith to believe that what God had said, He was more than able to perform. Yet, with each physical test, a spiritual test was a part of the package. Victory in one area gave way to what seemed defeat in another. So, what was a new mother to do? Get the prayer warriors on the case. Did that. Go to the altar for prayer. Did that. Read

From Mourning to Morning:

the Word. Doing that. Yet, it was a struggle not to entertain the enemy, as he began planting seeds of fear, doubt, and defeat in my mind. Then it happened—I was unaware of the severity of the problem. I went in to the hospital for another series of tests. I came home expecting to await the results; however, by the time we had gotten home, there was a voicemail from my doctor stating that she wanted me to go to the hospital immediately. I felt fine. I was obedient, and when I arrived on the maternity floor, the nurses whisked me into a room, changed my clothes and hooked me up to a baby monitor. My blood pressure had sky-rocketed, and I was in labor. No, this cannot be happening; my baby is not due until October.

It was August 28, 2000. The next couple of days seemed like an eternity. Then, the unthinkable happened; I was going to go into surgery. My son was born, August 30, 2000. Our little bundle of joy was here and although he was premature, he had all of his limbs. We were truly the proud parents. The next couple of weeks were critical for our son. Mom was in the hospital recovering from surgery, our little boy was in the Neo-Natal Intensive Care Unit (NICU), and dad was taking care of everything. Brian and I celebrated our wedding anniversary in the hospital, as well as his birthday.

It was Sunday, September 17, 2000. I had a pressing need that Sunday to go to worship. I needed that corporate worship to reenergize my spirit. Little did I know that God was preparing me for the road ahead. My cell phone rung in the service; Brian called and said, "Little Brian has to go into emergency surgery; I will meet you at the hospital." Our baby boy was strong, and on his last day on earth, he smiled at his father just before he was to go into another surgery, as if to say, "I am at peace, for I am going to be with the heavenly Father." I made it to the hospital and found Brian in the waiting room. "He is already in surgery." My heart sank. The next time I would see my son was in the NICU as we awaited the angels to take him home. Two days after Brian's birthday, our son went to be with the Lord. He had survived jaundice and one surgery that took a part of his colon. Words cannot express the pain that we felt that day and the years that followed. As King David had to do, we found ourselves in the same position. We had to get up, wash our face, and worship our Lord. We had to realize that we would see him again. It was during this time of reflection and meditation that the Lord spoke to me clearly about my destiny. He told me that I would have to teach through my pain. He told me to write in my journal. As I began to write, He would give me poems from the throne. He gave me songs. He showed me that He had not forsaken me. I don't know why my child had to die, but I do know that promotion comes through pain. The poems that are in this book are inspired by the Lord. My prayer is that, as you read them, they will minister to your soul. No matter what type of loss you have suffered, know that crying may last for a night, but joy truly comes in the morning.

From Mourning . . .

Crying may last for a night, but. . . (Psalm 30:5)

From Mourning to Morning:

Grief

Grief is like the fading leaves
It drops off and decays in the ground.
It is ever changing from gold to brown
It is like the storm that sweeps through the town.
Turning over everything in its path
Then Quiet-Still—It does not last.
The time it takes to walk it through—
Is totally up to you.
Pull back the clouds and let the warmth of the Holy Ghost
shine through.
Let Him put on the garment of praise.
Praise Him in it and through it all
For weeping may endure for a moment . . .
But as that moment lingers, pull on the strength you gain in
Him.
Joy cometh in the morning.
The morning will come.
Expect it. Expect it. It will come.
The morning is that moment when peace is still.

Scripture References
Psalm 30
Isaiah 53
Matthew 5
Revelation 21

From Mourning to Morning:

Due Date

My little angel was due today.
Yet, he came another way.
August 30th was the day.
Way too early, but no one is to blame.
It did not matter how you came.
You made it through just the same.
Eyes twinkling brown, hair so curly and smooth,
Your body so tiny, sculpted, shiny and new.
You cried so brief when they whisked you out from me.
Not by natural means, but by surgery.
Your father was so proud of you.
I was too.
We loved you so much.
This gift so fresh and new.
October 27th would not see you.
You were our little angel.
Sent for such a time as this.
So brief your stay yet you had a way of telling us Mom,
Dad, I'm going to be okay.
Triumph went to tragedy, in a blink of an eye.
Your little soul was preparing to fly.
Fly to the place where all men long to be.
Their home on high with Jesus the King.
October 27th is today.
I often wondered how it would have been.
A natural delivery. Joy in the pain.
Yet, today we stare at an empty crib.
I can hear your tiny voice saying
I just made room for another kid.
A sister or brother only God knows.
But a date with destiny they will have.
August 30th was mine.
To be with you for a short time.

From Mourning to Morning:

Don't be sad, discouraged, heavy or bound.
For I am growing up in the presence of our Lord.
Playing with other little angels, watching over you.
I felt your love. I felt your dreams for me.
I fulfilled my purpose although brief.
Don't mourn too long.
Be at peace.
I will see you again.

From Mourning to Morning:

Questions

I often sit and wonder why
Why Lord did this have to happen to me?
I look around and wonder how
How can this happen, why here and why now?

I often reflect on when
When will my breakthrough begin?
Sometimes I question out loud.

What's next?
Who's next?
Where will the POW hit and how?

A still little voice calmly comes in my mind.
Don't always question me, my child.
For I am the Lord, who sits high and looks low.
No need to wonder, I know.

I was there with you, I saw it all.
What you forgot is I too experienced the blow.
I lost my only Son too.

Just so that you could live and your children too.
Don't give up, Don't give in
No more questions
Just choose to Win!
Make this choice and all of your questions will end.

Scripture References
Psalm 71
Proverbs 3
John 3

Tests

Tests in school, it strikes fear in a child who is unprepared
It is those daily roadblocks that we do not share.

It can come out of nowhere.
One thing is sure, tests will come and go.

Whether you are ready or not.
God is saying, you do not have to cheat,
For if you do, I will not have them to stop.

So — get prepared, by reading the Word
Stay in prayer
When it comes you will not be unaware.

For you will have been truly prepared.
And success, yes sweet success
Because the tests have already been won!

Scripture References
2 Timothy
James 5
1 Peter

From Mourning to Morning:

Waiting

Waiting, Waiting, Waiting
Timing, Timing, Timing
When will the waiting be in the right timing?

I cannot begin to whine. Be strong and of Good courage.
The vision will speak
But you must wait for your time.

Wait for the Timing
God will not deny me—
Wait and not Fear
He is truly near

Wait and not Faint—
Do Good, Not Evil
Wait and Just Think—

Settle down, Settle down, Settle down
Wait—
God is still speaking
Just Wait, You will endure
You will succeed,
Stay on your knees
Just Wait . . .
It will soon be a brighter day.

Scripture References
Psalm 37
Isaiah 40
Lamentations 3
Galatians 6

From Mourning to Morning:

Will I Ever Smile Again?

At times it seems as if my smile has gone,
To a place where no one knows
Not even me.

I feel it trying to breakthrough
Like the sun upon the mountain dew.
Like a rainbow after a horrendous storm.
It stays hidden.
Is it really gone?

Will I ever smile again?
Not a fake show for my friends.
No one, not one knows why it left.
I do, my heart is shattered.

Shattered with the hope of the future.
Torn from my grip. So unfair, so cruel, too soon.
How can I smile again?
Will you tell me please?

You who have stolen from me.
Stolen my hopes, dreams, and a very special part of me.
You who have used me for what you wanted.
Now you ask me what is wrong, to smile.

Hell is where you are from.
Sent to steal, kill and destroy.
You who are known by different names.
But your mission has never changed.

To distract, take away the smiles
Of us who are doing—doing all we know to do.
Doing what we have been called to.

From Mourning to Morning:

Again, I ask—Will I ever smile again?
A rhetorical question.
I know the answer. I hold the key.
I know the Master, who is the Greater One in me.

Yes, the sun will shine again.
Because the Son is the one holding my hand.

From Mourning to Morning:

Smiling Through the Tears

Here I sit reflecting on my life
Some things have been wonderful
Others made me cry.

I often wonder how tragedy changes a man
Will it turn out for the best?
Is it truly in God's hand?

My flesh screams out why me Lord!
How can a servant of yours continue in their pain?
I smile, while all the time my heart is in chains.

I smile and give the polite response
Raise your hands; lift your head—God understands.
He knows your heart.
As the silent tears can no longer be disguised.

Lord, Jesus, Prince of Peace
Help me not be defeated.
Family, friends will never really know.
Just how deep my pain goes.

It seems as though there is a bottomless cup
Where my tears just flow from my tear stained heart.

I smile, to act as though those things which are not
are as they should be.
Lord, sweet Jesus—who cries for me?
Where is my Aaron, Naomi, Jonathan?
I am in dire need of open heart spiritual surgery.

From Mourning to Morning:

A transfusion of God's saving grace—
I thank God for His blood.
Yet, I continue to smile through my tears.

Scripture References
Psalm 56
Psalm 126
John 11
Revelation 21

A Heart's Destruction

    Sometimes a loss may make you feel as though your heart is totally destroyed; however, a heart's destruction is a perfect opportunity for God's reconstruction. Like a house that has busted pipes due to water damage. Everything in the inside appears ruined, yet you are able to recover your precious things. On the outside the house looks the same, but everything on the inside has been rearranged, purged and made new. The foundation is strengthened, and you are able to upgrade the things that you lost. That is how God works. He never tries to replace the old, but He provides you with something brand new. A new opportunity, a new start, a new outlook on life. The newness of the thing which was lost is the best that He always had for you. Remember, God specializes in fixing broken things.

A Broken Heart

A broken heart
Has been mended
Although the Memory is still there
I can still choose.

Freedom

Freedom comes with a heavy price.
Oftentimes, it may cost you your life.
Giving things up that you don't want to say.
Could cost you your freedom if you stall and delay.

God grants us His freedom when we come unto Him.
You can defeat the enemy, if you turn and repent.

So always remember that your soul is at stake.
But freedom, sweet freedom
Is awaiting you today.

Scripture References
Psalm 34
Psalm 147
Galatians 5
John 8

From Mourning to Morning:

Forgiveness

The Lord says for us to forgive
Yet the flesh is hard to give
Backstabbers, liars, player haters
They say they love you yet their hearts are black.

Always wishing that you fall out flat.
Flat on your—Ask God to forgive you, but you can't forgive others.
Yet, they say they love you like a brother.

A brother in the word, yet their heart is black.
Filled with envy, and no respect.

They shout, dance, wave and clap their hands
Yet, there is no heart change.

They cheer on the pastor in service.
"Amen brother," they yell.
While all along heated envy, raging hell
Is festering in the deepest innermost parts of their soul.

Forgive, for You I live.
Seventy times seven is my part.
Yet it is not in my heart . . .
I know that I must or I will not see His face.

Help I cry out.

No answer.

From Mourning to Morning:

Scripture References
Psalm 86
Psalm 103
Mark 11
1 John 1

From Mourning to Morning:

Think It Not Strange

Think it not strange
The events that go on
The bombings; killings; the devastating storms . . .

Think it not strange
The sorrows in life
The death; near death; with all of its strife.

The focus is clear
Can you hear the call?
Get your life right with Me
Come one, come all.

I love you my children
I desire all to be free
Don't you hear me calling?
Please choose Me.

I can and will give you eternal life.

Think it not strange
The truth is clear.
You have been blinded, by the deceiver
He is always near.

Open up your heart
Let Me come in.

Then you, too, will be a stranger in this foreign land.

From Mourning to Morning:

Scripture References
Psalm 95
Matthew 24
Mark 13
Luke 21
Hebrews 3

From Mourning to Morning:

Be Still

Children—Be still.
Search out the quiet times of His voice.

Listen for a call.
You cannot deny.
He calls.

Children—Be still.
Feel the coolness of time.
Brushing against the side of your cheek.

No movement, no movement.
Just resting in Him.

Shades of purple and blue in the sky.
A melody of grace is floating by.

Children—Be still.
Don't rush His grace.
Let the King of Glory
Have His way.

Scripture References
Psalm 46
Exodus 14

From Mourning to Morning:

A Quiet Place

I must get to a quiet place.
The place where you speak to me.
I must get to a quiet place.
Where there is always peace.

What is this quiet place?
This thing that I long and need.
A place where you speak just to me.
To me. To me. To me.

Who is in this quiet place?
A place I long to be.
A place where stillness reigns, joy abounds, no more pain.

My Lord Jehovah, Abba Father, Prince of Peace is in this place.
He is this place.
The quiet place, it's my heart.
The place where Jesus lives.

Getting to this place is as easy as a prayer.
Yes, beyond the veil.
In the presence of my Lord.
I seek His face.
Yes, that is how I get to that quiet place.

Scripture References
Psalm 23
Psalm 42

Christ-Like

What does it mean to be Christ-Like?
Do we really know?
Is it a tall order?
Don't we still have to grow?

Christ-Like is a process.
That gets easier with time.
We cannot be perfect, but perfected
That is our Christian line.

Perfected in the image of our Lord Jesus Christ.
Being able to handle the adversities of this life.

Being able to be humble when others sing your praises.
Being able to stand tall when surrounded by
liars and haters.

Being able to love, when by man's rules you should hate.
Being able to work hard when others seem to skate.

Christ-Like is a tall order indeed.
Yet, we do not become Christ-Like in our own might.
It takes the Holy Spirit to transform us into God's light.

Scripture References
James 1
1 Peter 3
Matthew 5

From Mourning to Morning:

The Presence of God

The presence of God is as near as a prayer
Focus, listening, silent, be still.
It is a place where only He exists
No more fighting, doubting, a sacrifice.

In His presence there is fullness of joy
His Shekinah is there forever more.

The world cannot get into this place
Neither can doubt, trickery or being fake.

Be real with God, He will be real too.
For in His presence, He is looking just for you.
The presence of God is as near as you want it to be.
The responsibility is on us to get back to this place.

The spot, the garden, where He dwells and walks.
His presence is as near as a shout and a cry out.

Jesus, Master, help me now
If you don't I will not make it,
No way, no how.

Scripture References
Psalm 16
Psalm 68
Hebrews 9

From Mourning to Morning:

Led by the Spirit

God lead us and talk to us
God lead us and breathe on us
No more doubting, fighting, or fear
We want your presence to be near.

Flesh you must die
In order for us to fly and move with Him.
We must be led by His Spirit.

Flesh you no longer rule
No longer will we be fooled
Tricked, tempted, and ruled by you.

We have grown; We are ready to eat the meat.
Led by the Spirit.
No longer in defeat.

God heal us, have Thine own way
Lead us, and guide us today.

Scripture References
Luke 4
Romans 8
Revelation 2

Thankful

Thankful I am for life
Thankful I am for strife
For it is in the time of strife that God has spared my life because He cares.
Thankful I am for family
Thankful I am for me
For it is time with family that I can truly see that it is all right to just be me.

Thankful I am.

Peace

What is Peace?
This thing called Shalom.
It is a quiet, still knowing in your bone.

What is Peace?
This good will toward man.
It is a smile, a nod, a yes you can.

What is Peace?
Will I ever know?
Yes my child, as you go your miles, and I call you home.

But until then, just rest in Me—And your days of struggle will turn to Peace!

Scripture References
Psalm 50
Psalm 100
Philippians 1
Philippians 4

From Mourning to Morning:

Praying Mothers

God has given us a special gift.
He has placed you in our midst.

Women faithful, strong and true.
Whose intercession for the Saints is sure to breakthrough.

Reflections of His love come in your smiles.
Kind words, A hug to get us through our trials.

We thank God for you everyday
Yes, we too, must now pray.

Our prayer is for God's face to continually shine upon you
And that He rewards your faithfulness, too.

For only what we do for Christ will last
So, mothers continue to take your stand
Keep marching in Zion's band.
At the end of the day, you can truly say
Your prayers made a difference in this foreign land.

Scripture References
Exodus 20
Proverbs 23
Ephesians 6
James 5
1 Thessalonians 5

From Mourning to Morning:

He Is a Friend

God is my friend
He longs to hear my heart.

True to the end
He will never leave or depart.

Man will always fail
He will use and abuse a pure heart.

God will not lie
His word will not return void
My heart cannot be shy
To express my faults, grief, and shame.

I rely on His strength and Blood.

God is my Friend
He will be yours as well
Give your life to Him or spend eternity in hell.

Scripture References
Proverbs 17
Proverbs 18
Proverbs 27
John 15

From Mourning to Morning:

The Greatest Gift

The greatest gift is Love
This we all have heard
But did you know—that you will reap what you sow?
So, sow what you want to grow.
If you want peace, plant it
If you want friends, be one.
The greatest gift you can give this season is your life to Christ,
For He is the Reason for All Seasons
And this is the greatest gift!

The Will of God

Do we really know the will of God?
The answer is a resounding YES
Read His Word
Seek His Face
Listen to His Voice
Still and Quiet.

From Mourning to Morning:

A New Beginning

With Every New day—God has given you—a new beginning
With the Breath you take—God has given—a new beginning
With every way that has been made—God has given—a new beginning
What you do today will determine your new beginning
Don't waste your new beginning, by being concerned about temporal material things.

Reason—Time Doesn't Wait For Any One.

Scripture References
Proverbs 17
1 Peter 4
Isaiah 43

From Mourning to Morning:

Love

Love is something that all seek but some will not find.
Love is a spirit not a feeling.
Love is the air that wisps across your face.
Love is the smile of a child of all colors and faith.

Love is not to be boxed in, marketed, and taken for a cheap spin.
Love cannot be brought, bribed, sold.
The love of man in this day waxes very cold.

Jesus, God, and the Holy Spirit are here to say . . .
We love you man
We love you woman
We love you children
So why are you acting this way?

Stop the killing, start chillin'
Start loving in the way that we have destined.
Yet sin has gripped your heart, torn it apart.
So now it has to mend, so you can begin to live again.

And at the very end . . .
Our love will win.

Scripture References
John 3
John 13
Romans 5
1 Corinthians 13
Galatians 5
Ephesians 5
Romans 8
1 John 4

. . . To Praise

Joy comes in the morning (Psalm 30:5)

From Mourning to Morning:

Worship

Worship is an act of your will
Sometimes it will take quietness
Be still.

Sometimes a shout, clapping of hands
Others will cry, kneel, or stand.

God lives in our worship
He loves to be Praised.

It is your heart that He's after
Won't you give it today?

He is looking for trueness, our spirit He craves.
It is all about Him.

Not how loud we can shout or how pretty we dance.
He just wants us to give Him a chance.

Worship is costly
Count the costs, do the math.
In the end you will see that only what you do for Christ
will last.

W-illing
O-bedient
R- everence
S- incere
H-oliness
I-ntegrity
P-raise

From Mourning to Morning:

Scripture References
Exodus 34
Psalm 29
John 4

Lord I Worship You

Lord I worship you
Lord I worship you
I give you the honor
I give you the praise

Oh, Lord I worship you
Oh, Lord I worship you

Lord I praise you
Lord I praise you
I give you the honor
I give you the praise

Oh, Lord I worship you
Oh, Lord I worship you

You alone are worthy
You alone are worthy

Oh, Lord I worship you
Oh, Lord I worship you.

From Mourning to Morning:

Hallelujah

Hallelujah, Hallelujah!
Hallelujah, you are worthy to be praised
Lord we love you and Adore you
You are worthy to be praised.

You are our strength
You are our peace
It is well; It is well with our soul.

Hallelujah, Hallelujah!
Hallelujah, you are worthy of the praise
Lord we love you, and adore you.
You are worthy to be praised!

No one can do more
No one do we adore
No one is mighty as you
You are worthy to be praised.
You are worthy to be praised.

From Mourning to Morning:

I Have Need of Thee

I have need of thee
I have need of thee
Lift up your holy hands
Lift up your holy hands
I have need of thee.
Oh, I have need of thee
Lift up your heart and Learn of Me.

Some love riches
Others gold, but my dear children
Now behold. I have poured out my grace.
Given you strength for the race.
I have need of thee.

Look up to my cross
Look up to my cross
Never look back and doubt.
I will always bring you out.
Look unto the King.
He is your Holy King.
He has need of thee.

Every joint will supply.
Every joint will supply.
I can't do it alone.
I created you for my own.
We must do each his part.
To be worthy of my heart.
I have need of thee.

From Mourning to Morning:

I Belong To You

When I wake up in the morning
Sun shining bright
I long to give you glory, for keeping me through the night.
I know you are with me
I know that you care.
'Cause you alone are worthy
My Father and My Friend.

I, I, I, I belong to you.
You are worthy,
I, I, I, I belong to you.
I love and worship you
I, I, I, I belong to you.

You give me peace, when I've cried all night
You are my shelter, in my storms and my fights
I know you are with me
I know that you care
I love you forever, You're always there.

I, I, I, I belong to you.
You are worthy,
I, I, I, I belong to you.
I love and worship you
I, I, I, I belong to you.

Your love is with me
Your presence is near
I know I can count on you
Through thick and thin

From Mourning to Morning:

I, I, I, I belong to you.
You are worthy,
I, I, I, I belong to you.
I love and worship you
I, I, I, I belong to you.

From Mourning to Morning:

Praise Unto Your Name

Praise, Praise, Praise
Unto your name Oh Lord

Praise, Praise, Praise
You are worthy.

Praise, Praise, Praise
Unto your name Oh Lord

Praise, Praise, Praise
You are holy.

You Oh Lord are mighty
Majestic in all your ways.
You are the King of Kings
That's why we give you praise.

Praise, Praise, Praise
Unto your name Oh Lord

Praise, Praise, Praise
You are worthy.

Praise, Praise, Praise
Unto your name Oh Lord

Praise, Praise, Praise
You are holy.

You Oh Lord are holy
The angels bow down and say
Holy is the Lamb of God
He lives and reigns today.

From Mourning to Morning:

Activate Your Gifts

Activate your gifts
Don't set them on the shelf
Start out doing something
Gifts can't motivate themselves.

Activate your gifts
Put your hand to the plow
Time is running out
Stop asking How.

Activate your gifts
Thousands are awaiting your debut.
Don't leave this earth without your light shining through.

Activate your gifts
God gave them just to you.
In His awesome plan, He had you in His hand.

Activate your gifts.
Boy, Girl, Woman, Man.
No more excuses
We are all a part of the Divine Plan.

It is up to each of us
But on the day of judgment
When we answer for all we have done.
Will you hear, Well done or Will you hear
Undone, my unfaithful one.

Scripture References
John 14
Philippians 4
1 Corinthians 12
1 Corinthians 14

From Mourning to Morning:

A New Woman

The Lord has made me a new woman
Full of Joy, Full of Peace, Full of Him
You see, the old woman, was grieved
Was doubtful, was not free.

Yet the new woman was only a prayer away
Just a silent moment, in a noisy day.
This new woman is Free, Faithful,
Happy To Be.

What made the change, you ask?
The Lord cleansed the heart, purged the junk
So He had room to work.
Old attitudes, hurts, anger, fear, stuff that had been there for years.

In a single, silent moment, In a noisy day,
He gave me a new heart, He took the Junk Away!

So, If you want to be a new woman
It is only a prayer, breaking moment
In a noisy day . . . away . . . away . . .

Scripture References
Joel 2
Luke 9
1 Corinthians 15
2 Corinthians 5
Colossians 3

From Mourning to Morning:

The Call to the Women of God

Mother, sister, daughter, wife
The road has been paved
God has shown you the way.

The mission is now clear
He has wiped away your tears.

Be steadfast, unmovable; abound in His love and grace
You must fulfill the calling he has placed over your life.

Time out for excuses
Obedience is better than sacrifice.

Scripture References
Exodus 23
Deuteronomy 28
1 Samuel 15
Isaiah 1
Romans 5
1 John 3

Epilogue

It has been six years since our son has been with the Lord. We are expecting God to do just as He said. In the meantime, we are walking in the calling that God has spoken over our lives. Not perfect, but each day being perfected. This one thing I know for sure, that God is on our side and my side, and when the days seem dark at times, I remember His promises for my life. I am determined to do all that the Lord has commanded me to do. So, now I exchange my garment of heaviness and sorrow for the garment of praise. I pray that in time you will too.

Decision

I pray that the poems in this book ministered to your soul. If you have never known the Lord, or knew Him and have been out of fellowship, the Lord is saying come home. There is nothing that you have done that God will not forgive. He loves you and you are very special to Him. Romans 10:9-10 tells us that "if you use your mouth to say, 'Jesus is Lord,' and if you believe in your heart that God raised Jesus from the dead, you will be saved. We believe with our hearts, and so we are made right with God. And we use our mouth to say that we believe, and so we are saved."

Please pray this prayer. *Jesus, I believe that You died for my sins and were raised from the dead. I ask You to come into my heart and be the Lord of my life. I confess that I am a sinner, and I ask You to forgive me right now. I receive Your gift of eternal life. Thank You, Jesus. Amen.*

If you prayed this prayer, heaven is rejoicing. Now the work begins. Pray and ask God to lead you to a place of worship that preaches and teaches the uncompromised Word of God, ask the Lord to fill you with the Holy Spirit, and be baptized in the name of Jesus. Now, grow in the grace and knowledge of our Lord and Savior Jesus Christ.

Reflections

From Mourning to Morning:

_____

_____

_____

_____

_____

_____

_____

_____

_____

_____

_____

_____

_____

_____

_____

_____

*. . . You will be sad, but your sadness will become joy.
(John 16:20)*

Reflections

From Mourning to Morning:

*I will praise the Lord at all times;
his praise is always on my lips. (Psalm 34:1)*

Reflections

From Mourning to Morning:

He gives strength to those who are tired and more power to those who are weak. (Isaiah 41:29)

Reflections

From Mourning to Morning:

_____

_____

_____

_____

_____

_____

_____

_____

_____

_____

_____

_____

_____

_____

_____

I lift my hands to you in prayer. As a dry land needs rain, I thirst for you. (Psalm 143:6)

Reflections

From Mourning to Morning:

*You are great and you do miracles. Only you are God.
(Psalm 86:10)*

Reflections

From Mourning to Morning:

Give me back the joy of your salvation . . . (Psalm 51:12)

Reflections

From Mourning to Morning:

_____

_____

_____

_____

_____

_____

_____

_____

_____

_____

_____

_____

_____

_____

_____

_____

There is a time to cry and a time to laugh. There is time to be sad and a time to dance. (Ecclesiastes 3:4)

Printed in the United States
202476BV00003B/19-69/A